Letters to My Loved One

A Grief Journal

Rasheda Randle

13TH & JOAN

For permission requests, write to the publisher, addressed "Attention: Permissions Coordinator," 205 N. Michigan Avenue, Suite #810, Chicago, IL 60601. 13th & Joan books may be purchased for educational, business or sales promotional use. For information, please email the Sales Department at sales@13thandjoan.com.

Printed in the U. S. A.
First Printing, October 2024
Library of Congress Cataloging-in-Publication Data has been applied for.
ISBN: 978-1-961863-96-5

This journal is dedicated to those in the "in-between."

In Loving Memory of My Mother, Tana L. Blackwell-Petty

GRIEF IS THE PRICE WE PAY FOR LOVE.

~ QUEEN ELIZABETH II

CONTENTS

PREFACE

I want to preface by saying that I am in no way licensed, educationally trained, or an expert in grief or grief counseling. I am, however, a person who has a lot of personal experience when it comes to grief. I am not here to counsel you in the technical sense. I just want to proverbially hold your hand while you navigate your own journey and share some of the things I've learned along mine.

My first memory of loss (as it relates to the death of a loved one) goes back to the age of 5 when my paternal grandmother passed away. When I was 10, a friend from school passed away from a tragic accident. Throughout my teenage and early adult years, I unfortunately attended many funerals of family and peers. I felt the impact of their losses, but I don't know if I really knew to grieve, let alone how to.

When I was 23, my mother suddenly passed away just days after her 50th birthday. Her funeral was the day before my birthday. Grief hit me like a freight train. I didn't understand it. I couldn't control my emotions. I didn't know how to navigate it. It was this loss that helped me to learn how to handle grief. So by the time I lost my beloved grandfather when I was 34, I was able to grieve in a healthy way.

I tell people all of the time...grief is a process. It's like living in a gray area, or as I call it, "the in-between." You're floating in this haze in between what your life was like before the loss and what it will be like after. Unfortunately, there is no cheat code to grief. There is no shortcut way around it, and trying to avoid it will only hurt you in the long run. The only way to get through it is to go through it. That is how you achieve peace.

There are five to seven stages of grief depending on who you ask, but for the sake of this experience, we'll focus on the five known as the Kübler-Ross model because that is how I learned to navigate grief. These stages are denial, anger, bargaining, depression, and acceptance (I call this stage "peace.") Reconstruction and recovery and the upward turn were added on later to create the seven-stage model.

Yes, there is truly a process to grief. But no one's process is the same. There is no real order to experiencing these stages, and there certainly is no timeline. While acceptance is the final stage of grief, one person may experience a stage before another or for a longer or shorter period of time. You may even feel more than one stage at the same time.

Because everyone copes differently, actions and reactions may look different from person to person. But in order to achieve peace or acceptance, it is important to allow yourself to feel every emotion and experience every stage. Most importantly, know when to seek help and find healthy ways to cope.

When my mother passed away, I was plagued with so much guilt that it basically drove my grief process. I teetered between stages, often revisiting them. I think I was planted in the anger stage the longest. Ultimately, my grief journey lasted seven years. You read that correctly. It took seven years for me to find peace in her death. At some point during my grieving period, I reached out to a therapist and began grief counseling. It was my therapist who suggested that I write a letter to my mother saying everything that I didn't get to say to her in life. Part of my guilt and anger was that my mother died with unresolved issues between us. I believe she had come to peace with them, but I had not. Because she had had those hard conversations with my sisters, but not yet with me. My therapist thought it would help to release some of the burden I had placed on myself if I had the conversation with my mother on paper. Tell her everything that was on my heart, and stash the letter away. So I did.

Little did my therapist or I know that one letter would turn into many. I started talking to her regularly through these letters, telling her about my day, rehashing our issues, reminiscing on our crazy adventures. To my surprise, this practice helped me to find forgiveness and ultimately, reach the final stage of grief.

That's what I hope this journal does for you. So often our loved ones pass away without us having the opportunity to make amends, get things off of our chest, or simply say "I love you." Or maybe we did and we just don't want the conversations to end. Maybe you're in the process of experiencing a loss and thus, grief has started early for you. Use the pages of this journal to write letters to your loved ones you've lost or are losing in whatever sense. Tell them everything you want them to know. Write a letter during each stage of grief you're experiencing, or just freestyle it day by day. Whatever works for you. While I can't promise it will make each day easier, I can promise that getting those thoughts and emotions out of the bottle of your mind will make each day a little more bearable.

Remember, there is no manual when it comes to grief. It is undoubtedly a painful and overwhelming process. I can only pray that this exercise will be a vessel in your healing and helping you find your peace, just as it was for me.

♡

With Love and Sympathy,

Rasheda

SHOCK AND DENIAL

ENIAL OCCURS IN THE EARLY STAGES OF GRIEF. IT'S LIKELY THE first one you'll experience. Why? Think about when you first learned that your loved one died or is dying, or when you've been faced with a great loss of another kind such as a divorce. In most cases, the first emotion you encounter is disbelief. You're in a state of shock, and you can't seem to wrap your mind around the loss. You don't want it to be true. You may feel an emotional numbness or as if the world has stopped around you. You may even feel some physical symptoms such as difficulty sleeping, lack of appetite, or nausea. Some may immerse themselves in work or something to keep them busy to avoid having to face reality.

I REMEMBER IT *like it was yesterday. I was returning home from work and my aunt, who lived down the street and had been watching for my arrival, called me as I was entering the house. "They rushed*

your mother to the hospital," she said. Before I could even hang up the phone, I was in my car racing to the east side of town. When I found my sisters in the hospital, they took me to my mother's room and I immediately stopped in my tracks. I couldn't feel my legs anymore. Who was this woman laying hooked up to all of these machines? That wasn't my mother. She didn't look like herself, and I had just seen her two days before at her 50th birthday party. There's no way.

The next two days in the hospital were a complete blur. I felt like I was having an out of body experience. When the doctor told us that she was brain dead and we had to make the decision to take her off of life support or let her be in a vegetative state for the rest of her life, I floated further into space. I don't even remember much from the hospital after that. I can't even recall her taking her last breath. Was I even in the room? Surely I was physically, but mentally, I wasn't there.

In the couple of days or so following, I thought I was doing myself a favor by attempting to keep myself busy. So I did what I always did. I went to work. I somehow made it through the morning news broadcast, where I was a member of the studio crew, but in the production meeting following the show, my team acknowledged my mother's passing. I remember running out of the room in tears. It was clear that I had tried to re-enter the world too soon.

Shock and denial are very natural reactions to grief. How are you coping with this stage?

_____

_____

If you could say anything to your loved one, what would you tell them? Ask them? Share with them? Use these pages to express yourself.

DEAR _____ ,

_____

_____

_____

_____

_____

_____

_____

_____

_____

_____

_____

_____

Dear _____ ,

Dear _____,

DEAR _____,

DEAR _____,

STAGE 2

ANGER

T HIS STAGE OF GRIEF IS PROBABLY THE MOST DIFFICULT TO PROCESS. IF you're a spiritual person, you may feel anger toward God – questioning why He would "allow" or "cause" you to lose your loved one. You may feel anger toward the person who is responsible for the loss. Or you may even feel resentment toward the person that you've lost – blaming them for leaving you. These feelings are not uncommon. It's how you channel them that's key. Lashing out at people, being violent or destructive are not healthy ways of dealing with your anger. But in total honesty, sometimes you just want to let out a scream, have a really hard cry, or break something. If that is what will give you a release, then do that. I am not, in any way, suggesting violence or destruction against self, other people, or others' property. But keeping that energy pinned up inside can lead to an explosion of emotion if it's not released properly.

Here are just a few ways to release anger in a healthy way:

- Write a letter to your loved one.
- Journal.

- ❖ Speak to a licensed therapist or join a support group.
- ❖ Scream (in private).
- ❖ Safely throw or break something (a rage room is a great place for this).
- ❖ Find an artistic release (i.e. writing a song or poem, painting or drawing).
- ❖ Verbalize your anger by venting to a trusted individual or speak as though you are talking directly to your loved one.
- ❖ Do a tough workout (boxing or kickboxing, high-intensity training).

I AM NOT PROUD *of the way I behaved during this stage of grief. I was simply not a nice person. I lashed out at everyone, got into arguments with my sisters, and even got pulled over by the police not once, but twice. The only reason I didn't go to jail is because both of the officers felt sorry for me. I just wasn't in a good headspace. My anger was being fueled by my own guilt, and I was taking it out on everyone else. I questioned God the most. I remember being livid with my sisters for scheduling our mother's funeral the day before my birthday. "Why would you do that to me? Why would you make me live with that memory?" They apologized and said they had tried not to have to have it on that day but because her funeral would be in another city, that was the only date available that would work. That didn't make me feel any better about it, but what choice did I have?*

I was angry at my mother, too. How dare she leave me with so many things left unsaid and undone? I remember being at the wake and having to ask my cousin's wife to keep me close to her and hide me from everyone. I didn't want to talk. I didn't want to be hugged. I didn't want people forcing me into an embrace when I was just trying to take a moment to myself. And I certainly didn't want to have to lie to one more person when they asked, "Do you remember me?" I was about to crack, and it wasn't going to be pretty. And you mean to tell me I had to do it all over again tomorrow at the funeral? God help me.

Perhaps what triggered me the most (and still does to this day) was all of the cliché phrases that people feel like they have to say when someone passes away. "It'll be okay...You have to be strong...She's in a better place." Listen, I know that people mean well when they say those things and that they likely say them because they don't know what else to say. But full transparency...no one wants to hear that. I surely did not. No, I'm not okay. No, I don't want to or have to be strong. Death sucks and I'm allowed to feel what I feel. Right now, I don't care that she's in a better place. She's not HERE where I can touch her, speak to her, embrace her. I'm allowed to feel selfish in this moment and want my loved one here with me.

This is where I learned that sometimes it's best to just be present with someone and not say anything at all. And, for the record, I refuse to say those cliché phrases to anyone anymore.

How are you coping with this stage of grief?

_____

_____

Dear _____,

37

DEAR _____ ,

Dear _____ ,

DEAR _____,

Dear _____,

BARGAINING

THIS IS THE STAGE OF GRIEF DURING WHICH YOU ARE LIKELY THE hardest on yourself and others. After a loss, you may start to feel helpless, desperate, or betrayed, which can lead to feelings of anger, guilt (including survivor's guilt), or anguish. As a result, you may end up judging or punishing yourself. Bargaining is, simply put, a defense mechanism used to combat those feelings. When you can't control the situation or you're struggling with accepting reality, you start focusing on what you or others could have done differently to prevent the loss of your loved one. *"If only I had taken him/her to the doctor a day earlier." "If only I had visited more."* You try to negotiate with yourself, with God or a higher power, or with others in hopes of preventing the inevitable or changing the outcome. *"I promise to be a better person if..."* Making deals or compromises become an attempt to try to make yourself feel better or lessen the loss.

I WON'T LIE, *this stage kicked my butt repeatedly. I mentioned before how my grief was driven by guilt. To provide some more context, I'll give you a little backstory as high level as possible. My mother was addicted to drugs most, if not all, of my life. But we were super close when I was a kid. One thing's for sure, she was going to tread hell and high water to make sure her baby girl was happy. My parents split when I was 12 years old and my sisters, who were both in their early 20s, took me in. Eventually I went to live with my father, but he struggled with trying to raise a teenage daughter on his own, and I definitely didn't make it easy for him. Ultimately I went back to live with my oldest sister, who kept me through college. I didn't make it easy for her either.*

Throughout my high school and college years, my mother was always there, somewhere, popping in and out. But she never missed a birthday, and never missed a holiday. Yet, still I suffered, and still do, from abandonment issues. I had built up a wall to protect myself from heartbreak, thinking, "If I don't let her get too close, it won't hurt when she leaves me again." This is a mentality that I carried into other relationships as well, but that's a story for another book. What I didn't know was that I was setting myself up for the ultimate heartbreak.

Fast forward to the year preceding her death. My mother was getting herself clean. She was doing so well. My middle sister had three sons and my mother was amazing with them. She was splitting her time between my sisters' homes. She would call me often to come and get her and spend time with her or take her to spend time with my paternal grandfather. But I always had an excuse. I worked two jobs and had a side hustle doing hair, so I always made myself too busy, which was a defense mechanism. I was still afraid to let her get too close.

In the week before her death, I had cut her hair in the style that she used to wear it in the 90s, and she was feeling and looking good, like her old self. September 13, 2007 was her 50th birthday. I was being my usual bratty self, complaining because she was late for her surprise party. I had other things to do before going in to work at 3 a.m. She showed up well over an hour later. I fussed at her for being late, hugged and kissed her, told her Happy Birthday, and left. That was the last time that I saw her alive. I missed her surprise engagement. I missed her opening her presents. I missed the speech she made about how happy she was to have her family back and how sorry she was for everything she had put us through. Thankfully my then brother-in-law caught it all on tape; but still, I should've been there.

Two days later, I got the call from my aunt. Two days after that, my mother was gone. So yeah, guilt had a field day with me. While she was in the hospital, I pleaded with God. I promised that I would be a better daughter if He would just let her come out of that coma. When she died, I judged myself by asking, "Why wasn't I a better daughter? Why couldn't I just get out of my own head and make time to spend with her? I made time to do anything else I wanted to do. I should have called her more. I should have visited her more. I should have been there. What really cut me deep was the fact that in that year preceding her death, she was able to have the hard talks with my sisters. They had forgiven each other and moved forward. I never got that chance. I was never going to get it. I was so busy trying to protect myself from getting as close as we once were out of fear that she would leave me again, and that's exactly what she did. She left me again. This time, forever. How was I supposed to live with that?

How are you coping with this stage of grief?

_____

_____

DEAR _____,

Dear _____,

Dear _____ ,

_____

_____

_____

_____

_____

_____

_____

_____

_____

_____

_____

_____

_____

_____

DEAR _____,

Dear _____ ,

DEPRESSION

T HIS IS QUITE POSSIBLY THE HARDEST STAGE OF GRIEF, AND ONE THAT can very easily last the longest. It's the stage where reality begins to set in and you start to truly *feel* the extent of the loss. Now you have to face the sadness, the hopelessness, and the emptiness. As a result, it starts to affect your everyday functionality. Isolation and withdrawal, weight loss or gain, lack of energy or interest in regular activities, restlessness, insomnia, crying spells, and feelings of self-pity are all common reactions in the depression stage. While the need to be alone is understandable and sometimes necessary, it is important to have a strong support system to help you through depression. It is equally important to cope with depression in a healthy way. Give yourself grace through this process; avoid developing a dependence on alcohol, medication, or any other potentially harmful substance. And don't be afraid to seek professional help.

AFTER THE FUNERAL, *my family tried to get me to celebrate my birthday by taking me out for dinner. I didn't even want to be out of bed, let alone celebrate my life when my mother had just died shortly after celebrating hers. I went, but I wasn't feeling it. Though I whole-heartedly appreciated all of the attempts to keep my spirits up, I just wanted to retreat. I just wanted to curl up in a ball and be left alone. And that's ultimately what I did, leaving the house only to go to work and for necessities.*

My sorority line sisters physically came to get me out of the house about a month or so later. They took me to dinner and then to a club. I wasn't ready, but I needed to have a little fun. That night out served as temporary gratification, but I was still struggling to operate in nor-malcy. I had mood swings, and I would often find myself crying just out of the blue. Grief is sneaky like that. One minute you're perfectly fine, and the next minute you have a fistful of tears. I had developed a dependency on Benadryl to help me sleep because I was so restless at night. I don't think I really knew that what I was experiencing was depression, but I knew that I was not myself. And I knew that I didn't like feeling how I felt. When did it end? When does the pain stop?

I decided to seek help. I reached out to a therapist through the EAP program at work and started grief counseling. It felt good to speak to someone who wasn't going to throw all of those cliché phrases that I did not want to hear at me and who was actually going to help me understand and decipher my emotions. I'd be back to normal again soon, right?

How are you coping with this stage of grief?

_____

_____

Dear _____ ,

Dear _____,

DEAR _____ ,

Dear _____ ,

DEAR _____,

ACCEPTANCE (PEACE)

THIS IS THE FINAL STAGE OF GRIEF. ALL OF THE EMOTIONS FELT IN THE previous stages of grief start to fade. The hurt and sadness become less and less with each day. Life doesn't necessarily get easier, but it becomes more bearable. Now you start to do the work, picking up the pieces of grief, preparing for "life after." You begin replacing painful thoughts with happier memories. When you speak of your loved one now, you can do so without sadness or pain in your heart, maybe even with a smile. You *remember* them, rather than *mourn* them. You start regaining control over your life. You start to accept the loss. You've found your peace.

IN ONE OF MY FIRST FEW SESSIONS, *my therapist suggested that in an effort to combat my guilt and anger, I should write a letter to my mother saying all of the things that I wanted to say to her but didn't get a chance to. At first, the task perplexed me. I imagined that part of the reason I never said what I wanted to say to her was because I didn't know exactly what to say or how to say it. And me, being the champion overthinker that I am, couldn't understand how writing a letter that would never receive a reply would achieve any type of res-olution. But I was committed to the task, so I started writing my letter. I must have started the first sentence over a hundred times. I recall bursting into tears because I felt that it was too hard and honestly, pointless. Then, in mid-cry, the words just came to me. They flowed out of me like my tears. I began to tell my mother everything that was on my heart. I cried again when I was finished. I felt so much better. I wasn't quite free from my emotions yet, but I literally felt a weight lifted off of my shoulders. That first letter ended up being five pages, front and back.*

I couldn't wait to get to my counseling session the following week to tell my therapist how grateful I was that he suggested this coping mechanism. By then, I had written more letters, one nearly every day, digging further into our unresolved issues or sometimes just catching her up on life. I kept this going for quite some time, even after my coun-seling sessions ended. Years after, actually. Life for me went on, and each day got a little easier to manage. I was, however, still in a depres-sive state. Holidays were still hard, crying spells would still occur out of nowhere or with any reminder of her. I would still get emotional sometimes when I spoke or thought of her. See, it wasn't uncommon for me not to see or speak to my mother every day or even every week. So in my mind, she was just out there in the world, living her life with her fiancé. I still had yet to actually acknowledge her death.

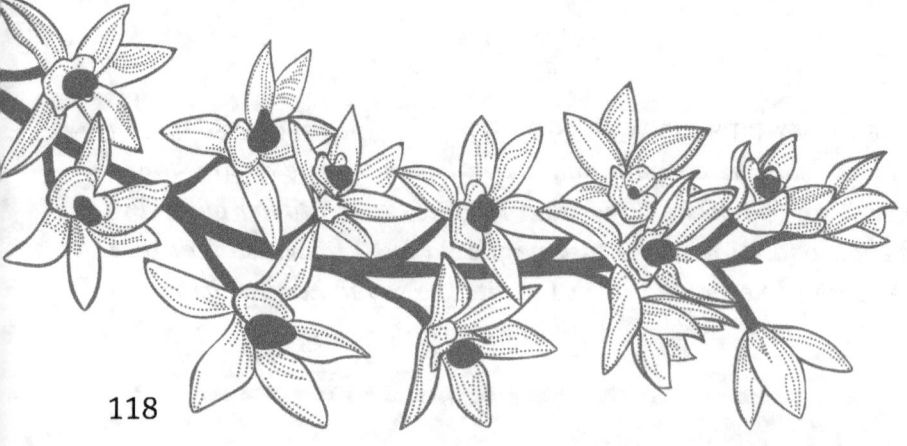

118

RECONSTRUCTION AND RECOVERY

A stage in the 7 stage model of grief. In this phase,
you begin to regain control of your life as you
are working through the aftereffects of grief.

In the years following, I tried not to think about grief so much. I slowly started trying to **reconstruct** *my life, but feelings from previous stages of grief were pulling me back. I had normalcy in my day to day but mentally, I needed to catch up. I started celebrating my birthday again; only now I was celebrating our birthdays. The last time I saw my mother was on her 50th birthday, and she was the happiest I had seen her in a very long time. That's how I wanted to remember her. And so birthdays became a big deal for me. I was getting to the point where I could tell a story about my mother and not cry or watch videos of her without a full-on breakdown. The pain of it all was subsiding. I was on an* **upward turn,** *but I was drifting.*

THE UPWARD TURN

A stage in the 7 stage model of grief. In this
phase, you begin to feel an emotional shift.
The pain and sadness lessen, your emotions
are not as intense, and grief starts to slowly
fade. Though it does not signify the end of the
grief process, you do start to feel some relief.

Seven years after my mother died, my aunt passed away and was buried right next to her. I hadn't been to my mother's gravesite since we buried her. (Well, I had. I just wouldn't get out of the car). I shocked myself when I actually got out of the car this time and took my seat at the burial site, feet planted directly on top of my mother's grave. I was shaking so bad, and not because it was the dead of winter in Indiana. As the committal service ended and everyone started going back to their cars, I didn't move. I couldn't. A family friend stood me up but still, I couldn't move. I just stood there, on top of my mother's grave. Before I knew it, I felt my knees buckle and I was on the ground, crying uncontrollably. I could feel our family friend right there beside me, trying to get me to stand up, saying, "Sheda, come on, get up. You gotta get out of the snow" or something to that effect. I distinctly remember hearing my cousin, who had just buried his own mother, say, "Leave her. She needs to do this."

I left everything in the snow at my mother's grave that day. All of the pain, anger, sorrow, guilt, depression, emptiness, grief...everything. I had finally found peace and accepted the loss of her. When I got back to Indianapolis, I wrote her one last letter:

Dear Mama,
I forgive you. I hope you have forgiven me.
Love Always,
Foosie

STAGE 5: ACCEPTANCE (PEACE)

How do you feel now that you've reached the final stage of grief?

_____

_____

_____

_____

_____

_____

_____

_____

_____

_____

_____

_____

DEAR _____ ,

As long as I can, I will look at
this world for the both of us.

As long as I can, I will laugh
with the birds, I will sing with
the flowers, I will pray to
the stars, for both of us.

~ Unknown

LIFE AFTER LOSS

WHILE LIFE AFTER LOSS MUST GO ON, GRIEF ITSELF NEVER REALLY goes away. It simply becomes manageable and you learn to coexist with it. So....

Give yourself permission to grieve.

Give yourself grace.

EPILOGUE

IN THE SEVEN YEARS OF MY GRIEF JOURNEY FOLLOWING MY MOTHER'S passing, she would show up in my dreams often. Sometimes she'd smile at me, but she never spoke to me. If I spoke to her, she wouldn't say anything back. She was just there. That is, until I reached the acceptance stage of grief. All it took was for me to come to peace with her death and now, she speaks to me in my dreams. I can actually hear her voice, her distinct laugh. It is so comforting. Sometimes our dream encounters are about something or nothing at all. But I find solace in the fact that I no longer need to write her letters. Whatever I need to tell her, we can talk about the next time I see her in my dreams.

GRIEF IS LIKE THE OCEAN. IT COMES
ON WAVES, EBBING AND FLOWING.
SOMETIMES THE WATER IS CALM, AND
SOMETIMES IT IS OVERWHELMING. ALL
WE CAN DO IS LEARN TO SWIM.

~ VICKI HARRISON

RESOURCES

REMEMBER THAT THE ONLY WAY TO GET THROUGH GRIEF IS TO GO through it and allow yourself to feel every emotion. Grief is sneaky, it's painful, and can sometimes feel unbearable. But that's not a journey that you have to travel alone. It is important to recognize when to reach out for support. It may be time to seek help if:

- ◆ You are having thoughts of suicide or harming yourself or others.
- ◆ Your feelings are interfering with your everyday life.
- ◆ You're experiencing intense emotions.
- ◆ You have a history of depression or mental illness.
- ◆ You are abusing drugs, alcohol, or any controlled substance.
- ◆ You've noticed no improvement after about six months..

There are a number of ways in which you can receive support. I've listed a few below, but there are a multitude of other options available with an online search.

- Check with your employer to see if they offer an Employee Assistance Program (EAP). This usually allows for a number of free visits with a licensed therapist and includes grief counseling.
- Check your local community for support groups. Some support groups are for certain types of grief or loss, while others are general and offer support for anyone who may be navigating grief.
- Online support groups and grief counseling, such as:
  - BetterHelp – www.betterhelp.com
  - Talkspace – www.talkspace.com
  - GriefShare – www.griefshare.org
- National Crisis Line: 1-800-273-8255
- Text HOME to 741741 or visit crisistextline.org.
- Dial or text 988 on your phone to reach the Suicide & Crisis Lifeline.
- Substance Abuse and Mental Health Services (SAMSHSA) National Helpline: 1-800-662-HELP (4357)
- National Mental Health Hotline: 1-866-903-3787

While you have reached the end of the book, you may still be processing the loss of your loved one and healing from your grief. My hope is that you will continue to use the tools introduced within these pages to find your peace. Specifically, keep writing letters and journaling all you experience as you heal. Use the following pages to express your range of emotions. Doing so will give you strength, courage, and the freedom needed to go forward.

RASHEDA RANDLE IS FROM INDIANAPOLIS, Indiana, by way of Evansville, Indiana. A woman of many hats and talents, she is an award-winning actress and an accomplished filmmaker, writer, director, producer, and now author. She is the creative visionary of Ivy League Productions LLC, and the founder of the Circle City Film Festival. In addition to her career in the entertainment industry, Rasheda is also a HR & HRIS consultant, project manager, and a licensed real estate agent in Georgia.

Rasheda graduated from Indiana State University with a BS in Radio/TV/Film. She was among the first graduating class of the music video production program at the New York Film Academy, and received her MBA in Marketing and Human Resources from Indiana Institute of Technology.

A member of Alpha Kappa Alpha Sorority, Incorporated, Rasheda currently resides with her beloved dog, Ivy, in Atlanta, Georgia.

Connect with Rasheda on Instagram (@officiallysheda)

www.ingramcontent.com/pod-product-compliance
Lightning Source LLC
Chambersburg PA
CBHW071324120626
46546CB00002B/426